# When God Speaks

Jackie Adeola Oni

I

# When God Speaks

ISBN 978-0-9553819-8-0

Step Out Creatives Publication,
Birmingham, UK

For copies of this book, seminars and fundraising
for the Schools Project in Africa, contact:
Email: Jackie_oni@yahoo.co.uk
Website: http://www.justgiving.com/GCE_LTD

Printed in Great Britain by Askew Design & Print
Doncaster, DN4 5HZ,
www.askewprinters.co.uk

Dedicated to
My mother &
brother

# CONTENTS

# INTRODUCTION

I have many testimonies, and one book will not be enough to write them all. God has been so good to me; that is why I have spent time to write these testimonies. This book is for young believers and non - Christians who do not believe that it is possible to have miracles in the life of a believer today.

It is expected that this book will edify and encourage many - so that they can see what God can do in an ordinary person's life. Moreover, they have to know how to put their faith firmly in our Lord Jesus who never fails. Hebrews 13:8 proclaims it: **Jesus Christ the same yesterday, and today, and forever.**

The words of the Psalmist in Psalms 37:25 are also comforting to my heart: **I have been young, and now am old; yet have I not seen the righteous forsaken, nor his seed begging bread.** This goes a long way to reveal how God has consistently been there for me, providing my needs and protecting me – because I made up my mind to hide in his righteousness, act according to his words, and listen to his voice. That's why God rains his miracles on me.

# APPRECIATION

I thank God for sparing my life and giving me the grace and opportunity to fulfil the promise I made to him in 1991 to write this book. I thank him because he is awesome, real, and dependable.

I would like to express my love and appreciation to my late mother Omolade Irene Sijuwade - a mother in Israel who dedicated her life to praying over the lives of her husband and children. I also thank my father for his love for us his children, and for giving us the opportunity to be well educated.

My profound appreciation goes to my loving brother Adetoro Sijuwade, who passed on to the world beyond, three months after the death of our dear and loving mother. In him, I found a very peaceful and caring character - synonymous to our mother in every way.

I appreciate the support of my dear husband Oluwole, my children Oyindamola and Temilade, for their love and encouragement through the years. I also thank God for my wonderful siblings who have been supportive and have been there for me through my experiences and dark times.

I will certainly not forget to thank all my spiritual fathers, mentors, and all those that God has used to encourage, teach, guide and touch me with great spiritual blessings along the way. They all deserve my deep appreciation.

I thank my editor and writing consultant, Isi Agboaye for his efforts and encouragement towards getting this book published. Finally, I am grateful to all my friends and work mates, for their support to my ministry towards reaching out to many children in Africa, (who are deprived of quality education) by helping to build quality schools for them.

# CHAPTER ONE

## TORMENTING BAD DREAMS

As a child, I remember always attending church every Sunday. It was also very important for us to attend devotion services at 6.00am and 6.00pm daily at home. During the devotion, we would read aspects of the Bible as a family and discuss what we read. It was very interesting. Easter was a very special period; and during this period, we would read many sections of the Bible, and devoted ourselves to God in prayers. Despite these Christian religious rituals, I went through my teenage years tormented by many bad dreams.

Most of the dreams were terrifying. I was not very happy about them and I longed for when that aspect of my life would disappear.  What was frustrating was that the dreams were very regular. I thought that they would never end, and was very worried about them and my mother was worried about how I felt.
In the dreams, I would see all sorts of creatures

chasing me. I would see big snakes that chased me about the place and I would get terribly scared, sweaty and panting as I woke up. Then I would switch on the light. This affected me so much that it became difficult to sleep with the lights switched off – especially in Nigeria where the electricity board, NEPA switches off power supply at will. People in the western world would hardly understand or believe that people can stay without electricity for hours or even days in our part of Africa.

Moreover, in some of those terrible dreams, I was bitten by dogs. The problem persisted in such a way that it took a great deal of my joy in my teenage years and shortly before I got married. It even seemed as if there would be no end to the suffering or the obstacles that the enemy put in my way; it looked like a torment that knew no end.

In some of the dreams, people pursued me; and this occurred several times. What was worthy of note was that as they pursued me, they would chase me into the house and suddenly disappear, turning into water. This really frightened me and I could not explain what this phenomenon meant. However, I could not conceal this experience because on such occasions, I would wake up with my heart beating very fast. The nauseating part of my dreams was that I was given food to eat - my native amala[1] with sauce, which was made of blood. From all indications, this was not a good experience and my heart was greatly troubled. Looking back now, I can see that the evil one wanted to spoil God's plan and purpose for my life. Praise God - the devil cannot destroy the plan of God for my life with his demonic antics. Thank God that he has always been on my side in spite of the plans and activities of the evil one.

> The LORD bringeth the counsel of the heathen to nought: he maketh the devices of the people of none effect.
> Psalms 33:10

As a result of my experiences, my mother went to many prayer people (called Aladura) to pray for me. It was the belief around us that such prayer people had the ability to cast out evil spells, knowing fully well that there was an evil perspective to my bad dreams. However, my experience with the Aladura – also known as the white garment church did not solve my problems.

---

[1] Amala. The paste is made with Yam flour in boiling water, and eaten with meat or fish sauce. It is popular among West Africans.

## A TURNING POINT

Some years later, God delivered me from those bad dreams because of the prayers and the counsel of various brethren. My brother in law, and his wife (both born again Christians) were very helpful. They were used by the Lord to encourage and minister to me through the word of God. Similarly, an evangelist friend and others prayed for me and spoke the word of God into my life. Moreover, I also personally became close to God - developing a close relationship with my Lord Jesus.

My experiences made me long to hear from God – I mean to hear God's voice speaking to me and directing me. Above all, I got so thrilled about the love of my Lord and saviour, Jesus. The reality and importance of John 3:16 dawned on me and this gave me great joy – that God gave Jesus to die for me and set me free from all sins and bondage.

> For God so loved the world, that he gave his only begotten Son, that whosoever believeth in him should not perish, but have everlasting life. John: 3.16

Taken literarily, this verse has been a great blessing to my life. I can see the impact of that love in my life – especially that God spared my life and gave me the courage to overcome those tormenting dreams. This verse also projects God's love. That God gave Jesus to the world to show his love – and if we only believe in that God of love, as shown by the risen Christ, we will not perish but have everlasting life. This was a great source of strength for me and I will never regret holding on to the love of God.

## DOES GOD SPEAK TO PEOPLE?
I had heard it said so many times, "God told me," or "God said" and I pondered deeply about this and once asked my brother in law, "How do you hear from God?" He certainly made an effort to explain it to me but I did not really understand his explanation.

Shortly after I got married, I then decided to be born again. At this juncture, it may be important to ask what it means to be born again. This is the process of having a changed life through the cleansing of the blood of Jesus, and the work of the Holy Spirit. Thus, this change is not by our human effort but by the help of God. Firstly, we have to confess Christ as Lord with our mouths, and believe with our hearts that he died for us and shed his blood to cleanse us from all sins so that we are fit to be children of God.

> Jesus answered and said unto him, Verily, verily, I say unto thee, Except a man be born again, he cannot see the kingdom of God.
> John 3:3

## DAWN OF AWARENESS

I realised people were able to hear directly from God and I started enquiring and questioning people about those bad dreams. That is how God delivered me, or rather, I got my deliverance. I wanted to be delivered from satanic attacks – I longed for deliverance so that I could serve God unhindered by the arrows of the enemy.

There is nothing as good as having a mind that seeks to ask questions. It is indeed a sign of maturity, development and an interest to move into greater heights with God.

> Ye have not chosen me, but I have chosen you, and ordained you, that ye should go and bring forth fruit, and that your fruit should remain:

that whatsoever ye shall ask of the Father in my name, he may give it you.

John 15:16

# CHAPTER TWO

## 'GIVE ME YOUR RAYMOND WEIL WRISTWATCH'

### AN EXPERIENCE IN GIVING

In 1987, I attended a Pentecostal church in Nigeria - a setting where I started speaking in tongues when I was prayed over. As far as I can remember, all through that day, I kept a sombre attitude, checking that I had not lost my ability to speak in tongues. As I read the scriptures, I gradually understood that mine was not a strange experience; that the Holy Spirit came upon the Apostles and they spoke in strange languages. I gained more confidence, felt at peace with myself and continued speaking in tongues privately.

A few Sundays later, at the same church, after the pastor had finished preaching, he asked us in the congregation to come forward and bring our offerings. My brother-in-law was sitting next to me. Suddenly I heard a voice say, "Give me your Raymond Weil wrist watch". I turned to my brother-in-law, but he was singing and not paying any attention to me. I thought to myself, "who is asking me for my one hundred and forty pounds wrist watch?" As there was no one on the other side of my seat, I asked my brother-in-law if he had said anything to me, he replied "No" - so I refused to give my wristwatch up but instead put some money in the offering.

## A CLEAR REVELATION

After the service, I went to wait for my brother-in-law in the church courtyard. As I spoke to some people, I saw an object that looked like a wristwatch. Surprisingly, it looked like mine and it was in on the floor – not knowing that my wristwatch had slipped off my wrist. The nearer I went towards it, the more it looked like the wristwatch I was wearing. As I picked it up, that same voice that I heard in the church during the offering said, "I could have taken this at anytime if I wanted to." I was immediately convicted; so I walked into the church hall, with the wristwatch in my hand and put it into the offering basket.

It was such an awesome experience. At first, it was amazing and a bit scary to be able to hear an audible voice, which I may describe like our normal voice – but however quieter and still. The fear of God came upon me and

the realisation that God is everywhere and
sees everything.

This single event has made great impact on my
life even as a Christian, until today. Moreover, it
has affected me in my walk with God and I
have come to realise that it is important for me
to do anything that God instructs me to do - no
matter how foolish it may look. I will do it
immediately, and not argue.

## OBEDIENCE IS THE KEY

God expects us to do many things that may
look foolish to many in the world – even
Christians. Many would laugh at you, thinking
that you have gone out of your mind. This is
where your faith counts; you must be strong
and know the God that you believe. Do not
shun your vision because of what people say,
how you feel, or what people do around you.
Be guided by the word of God at all times.

> Whether it be good, or whether it be evil, we will
> obey the voice of the LORD our God, to
> whom we send thee; that it may be well with us,
> when we obey the voice of the LORD our
> God.
> Jeremiah 42:6

A close look at the scriptures will reveal the fact that we are supposed to listen to the voice of God; and in doing this, we will be blessed – knowing that God operates at a higher level than us.

> 8 For my thoughts are not your thoughts, neither are your ways my ways, saith the LORD.
>
> 11 So shall my word be that goeth forth out of my mouth: it shall not return unto me void, but it shall accomplish that which I please, and it shall prosper in the thing whereto I sent it.
> Isaiah 55:8 &11

## GOD ARRANGED A LOAN FOR ME

I remember a period when I was very broke, and my credit was not good with the bank – meaning that I could not borrow any money from the bank. However, I kept worshipping and praising God. On this faithful day, God instructed me to leave the dishes I was washing, and he dictated the letter I was to write to my bank manager, requesting for a loan.

For those of you reading this, and are not in the western world, when you have a bad credit, you are automatically refused loan in the major banks. However, if you know deeply that it was God instructing you, you have to expect a miracle – including signs and wonders. DO NOT DOUBT. Play your part – do what God says, and God will complete the rest. Someone said that God puts the "Super" on your "natural" effort, making it "Supernatural".

I wrote the letter, and three days later, I got the loan. I was so joyous – so excited that I asked what I could do for God to express my thanks. The Lord then said I should write a book, about my Christian experiences for young Christians, and non-believers.

> 2 And the LORD answered me, and said, Write the vision, and make *it* plain upon tables, that he may run that readeth it.
> 3 For the vision *is* yet for an appointed time, but at the end it shall speak, and not lie: though it tarry, wait for it; because it will surely come, it will not tarry.
> HABAKKUK 2:2&3

# CHAPTER THREE

## "GO OUT THERE AND SAY, YOU HAVE A JOB FOR ME"

In 1991, I had left my job as an accounts clerk at Freemans – a mail order company. It occurred to me to start some business of my own. I was very excited to do this; however, God had not instructed me to do this. Months past, and I had no income coming in. About six months later, I started getting worried as my husband had to pay all the bills, and we had a baby as well. I was more disturbed because I also wanted to contribute something but I had no financial resources to do so. I felt disturbed that my husband was carrying the financial burden for the family alone – I just wanted to play my part. This certainly drove me to take action and I was looking unto God to direct me.

**A 'STUBBORN' FAITH**
One day as my husband left the house, I knelt down and cried out to God to help me. This

was about 3.00pm on a Friday and God said to me, "Go out there and tell them, you have a job for me" I thought to myself, I have absolutely nothing to lose, so I got dressed and left the house. On the way out, I met my husband, and told him what God had said. He replied,"You cannot do this, you should write and ask for application forms, and take your CV". I decided to take a leap of faith – in relation to what God had spoken to me.

On getting to the banks in the high street, I became very scared. Instead of saying, "You have a job for me", I said, "Do you have a job for me?" All the banks said ''No.'' It was then I remembered saying to God, ''well I have done what you have told me to do, and now it is up to you.'' I had one more agency to try, which was a secretarial agency (I was just desperate to do any job to bring money in), I decided to go to them as well.

As I got to the secretarial agency, they were locking up to go home. One of the employees recognised me, and asked if I had problems with my mobile phone – as she had been trying to contact me for the past two days. I replied that my mobile phone was faulty.  She then asked if I could do a bank job. I said 'yes.'

She spoke to the bank on her mobile phone

and they asked me to resume work on Monday – bearing in mind that it was Friday. This is how I got a job at Barclays Bank Plc. My husband could not believe how this had happened in one day. This was my transfer from Freemans Mail Order Company to the banks in the city of London.

> ...If ye have faith as a grain of mustard seed, ye shall say unto this mountain, Remove hence to yonder place; and it shall remove; and nothing shall be impossible unto you.
> Matthew 17:20

This single event strengthened my faith and made me believe in the fact that there is power in the word of God. As long as you know it is God that has spoken to your heart, you will not be put to shame if you listen, trust and obey his voice.

**WARNING THROUGH DREAMS**
Sometimes God may speak to you in a dream to warn you. I remember a day when I dreamt that my daughter in secondary school was knocked down by a car. In the morning, I called my daughter and told her to be careful when she was going about her affairs and prayed for her safety. At about 2.00 pm, my

husband phoned me, saying that a car speeding down the hill near my daughter's school had hit her as she crossed the road at the bottom of the hill. I was not worried, but asked how she was. He said that she actually bounced off the bonnet of the car; and to God's glory, she landed on the ground with no broken bones, cuts or bruises.

Coincidentally, that same day in another street, a car hit my daughter's classmate and she spent three months in hospital with broken bones. Praise God that my daughter was back at school the following day – praise God.

One sure way that you know that God is at work, is when you see great things happening around you, and you practically know that you had no part to play in creating the miracle. God did it all by himself and he deserves the glory. Many things are beyond your capability; but God works within our weakness to create great miracles. God is great!

> A thousand shall fall at thy side, and ten thousand at thy right hand; but it shall not come nigh thee.
> Psalm 91:7

# CHAPTER FOUR
# WHAT'S NEXT LORD?

Occasionally things may become quiet; meaning that you may not hear God speaking to you. You may wonder if God has left you, or if he is still with you in your problem. You may begin to doubt if you are still spiritual, praying as you ought to, or wondering if you have done anything wrong.

It was one of those days that a friend visited me at home. I asked God what was next. I said; "what is it you want me to do?" God said; "your husband's car." As I set about telling my friend who came to visit what God had just impressed on my heart, my husband came in. I asked my husband what he was doing at home so early and he said that he had problems with the car engine. I asked him how much it would cost to get a new engine. He told me, and God provided the amount for us. The next thing he said came as a total surprise and I knew that it could only be God.

## IT PAYS TO BE PATIENT
My dream car is Mercedes Benz; so I wanted to go to Germany to buy it, as it is cheaper there. However, any time I asked my husband, he wondered why I wanted to buy such a car. I therefore decided to be patient about it all. On this faithful day when my husband's car was faulty, and God had provided the money, my husband turned to me and said; "why don't we go to Germany and buy the Mercedes Benz?" Surprise - what I had given up on had suddenly come to life – my patience had paid off at last.

## THE MINISTRY OF GIVING
It is important to know what your God given ministry is. I believe mine is in the realm of giving and in many years of obeying God, I have seen and experienced sudden blessings. Blessings that make one go "Wow"!

This reminds me of a situation where I went to an Aunt's house only to see the very bad way she was living. This Aunt would serve us (her younger nieces) in our own homes and would make us laugh so much. Although I did not hear the Lord speak directly about this situation, my heart was heavy about my Aunt's living condition. Although I had no lump sum stashed away to give her, I told her I would help her build a house. Her landlord had sold her land many years ago at a discount and as such, there was something to use immediately.

I would send money to her and sometimes had to manage on a little amount to survive until the next payday. I ensured however that I paid all bills that needed to be paid - so nothing at home suffered financially because of the help I was providing my Aunt. Moreover, I did not rush out to watch movies or buy clothes for myself over those years. During this period, I was made redundant twice at work.

I reminded God that he had to do something for me – seeing that I was supporting others financially. To God be the glory, each time I was made redundant, I had a job immediately and I had a choice of three to choose from. This shows that when you obey God especially financially, the enemy would come in to disturb your programme – even the loss of your job. Praise God, the project was done as other siblings came in to assist and the building still stands – to God's glory. Hallelujah.

> Is it not to deal thy bread to the hungry, and that thou bring the poor that are cast out to thy house? when thou seest the naked, that thou

cover him; and that thou hide not thyself from thine own flesh?

Isaiah 58:7

# CHAPTER FIVE

## REVELATION OF A BRAND NEW OFFICE

Sometimes you never know how God will bless you or through whom he will relay a message to you. I received a gift of many cassettes by various Christian musicians from Africa. For some interesting and inexplicable reason, one particular cassette moved me deeply and spiritually whenever I listened to it. I was not only thrilled, but was greatly blessed and inspired when I listened to it.

Because of the positive and spiritual impact that I had from the music, I got in contact with the musician – an evangelist, who is now a good friend and as close as a sister. Meeting with her was such a great blessing and I instantly felt that many others should actually enjoy the benefit of her music and ministry. So I strongly felt in my heart that something practical should be done. That is how we arranged a musical concert in London and it was very successful. I was thrilled to put all my savings into that concert – an act that will baffle any sceptic. However, I knew that it was the will of God and that God's name will be glorified through the event.

## GOD WILL REWARD YOU

The point I am trying to make here is that there are certain things that we would like to do, but we shy away from doing them because of fear or lack of faith. I have come to see and learn that God sees all things and he will reward all acts of obedience to his voice – especially when the act of obedience is towards the propagation of his work. See 2 Samuel 24:24.

> And the king said unto Araunah, Nay; but I will surely buy [it] of thee at a price: neither will I offer burnt offerings unto the LORD my God of that which doth cost me nothing. So David bought the threshing floor and the oxen for fifty shekels of silver.

At the end of the day, I am willing to testify to the glory of God, and be an example to the saints of God. That is why I sacrificially gave most of my funds into the musical concert. This covered the cost for renting the hall, leaflets, radio advert, etc. As I did this act, I felt a sense of satisfaction and I asked God to use the concert to save some souls. Once again, I was told at work that my job was to end that week. I held on to faith and started applying for jobs. – trusting that God will see me through.

## A BLESSING IN THE CORNER

A few days after the concert, I was invited to a job interview. I called my evangelist friend and asked her to pray for me as I was on my way to an interview. Her response was "My God, I saw you in the spirit in a brand new office at a senior position." I asked her why she did not inform me earlier. She retorted that she did not know what my job situation was like, and did not want to intrude by asking me. Do you know that I got that job as an Assistant Manager at Commerzbank (a German bank)? To cap it all, everything in the building was brand new as we set up the London branch.

Be aware of the fact that as long as you have a right motive and your heart is right in the presence of God, he will sort your own situation out in an amazing way. I am always excited at the prospect of giving – knowing that in doing that, God always has a blessing in store for me. Thus, when God instructs me to give, I know from experience that a blessing is coming my way too. However, this is not to say that I am always looking forward to receiving from people when I give. In my experience, my blessing does not come from the person I gave directly to, but from other sources. See Luke 6:38.

> Give, and it shall be given unto you; good measure, pressed down, and shaken together, and running over, shall men give into your bosom. For with the same measure that ye mete withal it shall be measured to you again.

The word of God cannot lie; even non-Christians practice this spiritual fact and it works for them. Do you notice that when a product comes newly to the market, the first samples are given free to people at various city centres in England and even in some poor countries? Do you notice how people flock to purchase it afterwards? That is the power of giving in action.

> I will open rivers in high places, and fountains in the midst of the valleys: I will make the wilderness a pool of water, and the dry land springs of water.
> Isaiah 41:18

# CHAPTER SIX

## I SAW A PAVEMENT WITH RED FLOWERS

# JULY 1992

Have you ever noticed that sometimes you may receive a vision or a word of knowledge, and you decide to share it with someone else - but it may not be received favourably by the person that you are sharing it with. It even gets worse when you receive negative and critical judgement.

I once had a memorable experience with some friends (visiting with us) who believed that God would grant them favour to buy a flat in London. They had one week to accomplish their mission to buy the flat in London – so they visited many properties. Moreover, they would wake up early in the morning and pray – and their prayer points were centred on buying the flat and then return to their country.

One faithful day, I decided to join them in prayers. As we finished praying, I saw a vision of a front pavement lined with red flowers. That was all I saw.  I told my visitors what I had seen in the vision and they referred to the property catalogue if there was anything like that in it. The only picture that was there with red roses was exactly as I had described in the vision to them.

They decided to go and view the property only for them to tell me that I should check what I had seen in that revelation – saying that the property was not for them.  They even teased me that I only have to close my eyes for minutes and begin to receive visions, or hear God speaking to me. They continued by saying that no one in the Bible saw visions like that. You can imagine how I felt as a baby Christian, having been excited about what God had shown me.

The following day was the D-Day. The day the property was going to be auctioned; so my visitors earmarked two properties that they were going for. I went to work as usual and we all met in the evening back at home. My visitors looked sad and I therefore thought they had not bought any property.  To my amazement and to God's glory, they had bought a property – the one, which had red flowers in front of it. 'You guessed right' they said - they had bought that property which I had seen in the vision. To my amazement, they informed me that the two properties they were actually interested in had been withdrawn from the auction. God has not changed – the Bible says that he is the same yesterday, today and forever. Moreover, God will never lie.

> 19 God is not a man, that he should lie; neither the son of man, that he should repent: hath he said, and shall he not do it? or hath he spoken, and shall he not make it good?
> Numbers 23:19

The property is now worth six times its original value. I was excited to see that God was real in my life and they tried to explain to me why they originally felt the way they did, but it did not matter to me. What mattered was that God had justified himself through me, and as a result, that strengthened my faith in him even more.

The reason why I have used this illustration is to put few important points across to young Christians thus:
  a.  Do not let anyone put doubts in your mind – especially when God reveals something to you.
  b.  So long as you are hearing from God,

put your trust in him and not in mere people.

c. It may be wise not to say all you see or hear from God to just anybody; moreover, you may like to ask God to guide you to whom you ought to share your vision with. This is because people will take you for granted and frustrate the anointing of God in you.

The truth is that I had actually taken it for granted that everyone must hear from God the way I did. The visitor did not know she was prophesying into my life by saying "before you close your eyes you have heard from God or seen a vision" because that is exactly how God works in my life. Although I do not advocate this as an example – knowing that I encourage long prayers, I do not pray for hours on end before God speaks to me. I may sometimes talk to God for five to ten minutes and receive a message from him.

Note that we all have different gifts from God; so guard yours so as not to create unnecessary jealousy. Moreover, be careful so that you do not come into conflict with those whose line of ministry or vision does not fit with yours. God has a clear vision mapped out for you and that is the guideline that should help you through your ministry and life on earth. To cut a long story short, I was given the contract of re-decorating the flat. Have you learnt a lesson about holding onto your vision? God will always prove himself real in your life. Amen.

> Then said the LORD unto me, Thou hast well seen: for I will hasten my word to perform it.
> Jeremiah 1:12

# CHAPTER SEVEN

# SAME FLAT FOR FIFTEEN YEARS

## GOD, WHERE ARE YOU?

I believe in space – large spaces and I believe strongly that people should have enough living space to do whatever they like to do. In my situation, space was needed and would certainly be appreciated.

It was not easy for my husband and I – including two children to share a second floor two-bed room flat for fifteen years. Worse still, we always had people visiting with us; and it was sometimes not convenient but we did all we could as a family to share our little space. During this period, there were many redundancies and there was negative equity - meaning that what you owe in mortgage is a lot higher than what the house is worth. Thus, thinking of moving to a bigger house was out of our reach.

One day my husband told me that he had secured a mortgage from his bank and that we could start looking for a bigger place. My joy was so full. The excitement suddenly dried up as my husband, being a very practical person was more interested in houses that needed to be redone. That was not exactly where I thought God was leading us at that particular time – we needed to move higher.

## SURPRISE

There was a house that my husband found, but the children told me not to bother going to see the place – meaning that there was need for something else. I sat in my bedroom and wondered why after fifteen years we were moving to a place that was not up to scratch. Suddenly, I heard the door flap sound and I knew it was not the postman as he had already been. I went to the door to find a leaflet of a beautiful house for sale posted into our flat. It was very gorgeous, and the price was very reasonable - within our budget. I went to meet my husband at work and encouraged him to let us go and view the house. He agreed and I was very happy.

## A HOUSE FOR US

When we got there, our children were excited about the house – they knew immediately that this was the house for us. It was very suitable for us. The seller had all her belongings packed into boxes as a potential buyer had disappointed her. She was therefore ready to reduce the price so she could move out as soon as possible. This is how we bought an eight-year-old four-bedroom townhouse on three floors. The following year, a tram link was opened by our house – great! This increased the value of the house. God is forever faithful. He knows what we desire - he is a true father. See Psalms 90:17.

> And let the beauty of the LORD our God be upon us: and establish thou the work of our hands upon us; yea, the work of our hands establish thou it.

# CHAPTER EIGHT
## CAR BLESSINGS

As you may have noticed, the testimonies of my life are around material blessings; these are actual blessings that God has manifested in my life as I obeyed his instructions. I am sure you would like to know my secrets; it is tithing. That is it – tithing! This means giving a tenth of ones earning to the work of God. It even becomes more interesting when you give more than the tenth. You will receive more blessings – more favour from God, the provider of all good things.

### IT'S IMPORTANT TO TITHE
Most people may choose to joke when they receive instructions from God - not me. To show how important the subject of tithing is to me, I choose to pay my tithe by direct debit; and I am blessed to work in a place where my payment to a charitable organisation is amply rewarded. This means that the company I work for matches the payment I make. Because of this, my church gets much more. You should not be surprised when God rewards me

through material things. I just hope that you would rejoice with me and as you believe God, he will bring yours to pass – Amen.

> Bring ye all the tithes into the storehouse, that there may be meat in mine house, and prove me now herewith, saith the LORD of hosts, if I will not open you the windows of heaven, and pour you out a blessing, that there shall not be room enough to receive it .
> Malachi 3:10

### IT'S SWEET TO BE BLESSED

My first Mercedes Benz was bought in Germany and driven over here to the UK. It was so clean and nice that I was very happy any time I drove in it. I had driven the car for about two years. On one blessed day, I went to visit a friend, who at the time I arrived was seeing off her cousin. As I was parking the car, they were both coming out of the house. The cousin (whom I had never met before), said, 'I want to buy your car.' I told her it was not for sale and even thought she was joking. She kept asking me how much she should pay for the car. Being that I loved my car, I gave no reply.

The following week, my friend's cousin sent me a cheque for an amount just five hundred pounds less than what I had paid for the car two years prior. I decided to go with the flow but it meant I would not have a car. As I was pondering about this, I remembered my brother had a Mercedes Benz he wanted to sell, which he had bought in Germany. The car was a very slick sports car with air conditioning, auto seat belt, spoilers, etc. On several occasions, I had seen the car parked - but as I had my own car, I did not bother to enquire about the car. I told my brother what had happened regarding my car and asked him what he was doing with the sports car. His reply confirmed to me that God's hand was in it all.

## A SWEET UPGRADE

He told me he had been trying to sell the car for so long. As his wedding was approaching, he needed cash. So he sold it to me at two thousand pounds less than what he originally wanted, and at the exact amount that the woman was paying for my car. This is how I had an upgrade of my Mercedes Benz. Sometimes, when you think that God has finished with you, He suddenly opens more doors to your utter surprise.

A few years after buying the sports car, my children and I were going home from church one sunny day. I heard the Holy Spirit tell me not to go home but to go to a Mercedes show room near our house. I recall asking myself what I was going to do at a Mercedes show room – wondering that I did not have any money and that I am happy with the car I had. I told my children what I had heard and they asked how much the cars there were. I said they usually range around thirty thousand pounds and they asked if I had the money. I replied "No" but also said I will not be buying at that price but mine will be around sixteen thousand pounds.  I was not sure why I made that utterance. It must have been Holy Spirit inspired.

I instructed my daughters that when we arrive at the courtyard, they should look for a dark coloured car since I do not like light coloured cars. We also decided not to go and talk to any salesperson but just search for the car. It is important that when you hear from God to key in and take your family along on the dream/vision. It was easy for my children to key in to such, as they have seen God's work in our lives in the past. We got to the car courtyard and to the glory of God; we saw one beautiful dark purple car and agreed that it was the one for us.  As we looked closely at it, we saw that the tag stated the sum of sixteen thousand pounds. I jumped for joy – remembering that another brother had bought a similar car for thirty two thousand pounds; I just knew God was working yet again. I decided not to put down the one thousand pounds deposit until I discussed with my husband. The salesperson predicted that I would not find the car there the following day; stating that it was top of the range with a special price. I told him it did not really matter – but I assured myself that if God has reserved it for me, he would keep it for me.

I discussed it with my husband who wondered why I was always interested in Mercedes Benz. The next morning as I was about to leave the house, my husband decided to go and view the car. Surprisingly, my husband was able to bargain and get the price reduced to fifteen thousand pounds. Thank God for the business instinct in my husband – a great gift and blessing from God. We bought the car. I am driving the same car today. God is forever faithful to his children, and willing to show up in all situations.

Now he that ministereth seed to the sower both minister bread for your food, and multiply your seed sown, and increase the fruits of your righteousness;)
2Corinthians 9:10

# CHAPTER NINE
## MY MOTHER
## JUNE 2001

I will always remember my mother as a caring, loving person who did all she could to ensure happiness for others and especially her children. She was a woman who was very humble and carried herself in a respectful way. She would entertain anyone but was very glad to do the simple things in life such as read books and watch good movies. She also spent most of her life in one church or the other getting prayers for her husband and her children. I am grateful to God for having such a wonderful mother.

My mother suffered from diabetes and high blood pressure. Her situation eventually deteriorated and I had to travel to Nigeria to bring her over to London. On the night we were due to travel back to London, my mother went into a coma. It was one of those periods when there was scarcity of petrol in the country. It was also the morning of the thanksgiving for my father's retirement as a state judge. Therefore, we were expecting visitors from all parts of the country. Many would be stopping by enroute to the church.

I was in the bedroom with my mother and as I realised what had happened, I arranged for a driver to take me to collect her doctor at 3.00a.m. My mother's sister and other relations were in the room and they were all crying and fearing the worst. In all these, my spirit was not moved. I asked the driver to pray for her rather than cry. I cannot explain the amount of peace that flowed within me because I was so much at peace with myself.

There was no guarantee that I would meet my mother back alive when I got back, yet nothing made me feel anxious. The doctor revived her and gave us his blessing for us to travel. It was much later that he told me he never thought she would survive the trip and just wanted her to leave the world in my arms.

We arrived safely in London and a week later, she had an operation to remove an ovarian cyst. Great excitement greeted the successful operation and we all believed that God had given her a new lease of life. Our joy was greatly multiplied when my mother was offered a permanent stay in the United Kingdom.

We knew this would be a great advantage to her treatment, recovery and general well-being.

After the operation, my mother stayed with my brother and my daily routine was to go to visit her after work, everyday, before going back home. On one particular day, I was so tired and was not able to maintain my routine. Therefore, I decided to go home from work. The Holy Spirit told me to not to go home but to go and see my mother. Meanwhile, this was another instruction that I could not afford to disobey - so I went to see my mother.

My brother's house had a security system fitted in so that my mother is able to see anyone at the front door downstairs; so she would be able to press a knob near her bed to open the door. This was done to allow her to recover from the operation without going up and down the stairs from her bedroom.  With this device, it was possible for her nurses to come in easily and dress her wound. The caterer was also able to come in to give her food and keep her company.

**GOD IS FOREVER FAITHFUL**
My brother and sister-in-law have very busy work schedules and they arrived home quite late in the day. The day I got there, I pressed

the doorbell and heard my mother calling for help, as she was unable to get to the knob. I knew something was wrong but did not have the keys to the house. Instantly, God moved miraculously. I reached for my phone and called my brother – asking him where he was. He answered, "right behind you". I did not know how to express my relief as we rushed upstairs to find our mother on the floor. She had fallen down as she was on her way to the toilet and had been like that for about two hours; and this was soon after the caterer had left. We helped her up and I called the doctor who then called the ambulance.

My mother detested going to hospital and she was angry anytime she saw me calling the doctor. As soon as the ambulance arrived, my mother went into a fit and coma. We were later to discover that she had had a major stroke. As they got to the hospital, she was taken to the resuscitation room. My brother and I waited for what seemed like ages until she was revived (again) but was still in a coma. She was then moved to a ward where I kept vigil with her.

## WHOSE REPORT ARE YOU GOING TO BELIEVE?

The following day, there was still no change, no movement, and no sound. The consultant told me she would not survive to the next day due to her age. He said that even if she recovered, she would be seriously deformed and may not recognise us (her children) due to the major stroke. Even with the coma, I could see a side of her face had dropped compared to the other side. It was as though there was nothing else to do. I then invited my pastor to pray and give her the final rights.

As the pastor was praying, I heard the Holy Spirit say to me, "If only my children can humble themselves and pray, then will I hear them and answer their prayers." I knew immediately that was God talking to me as I did not know that Bible quotation and many others at that time, and could not have recited that myself. I stopped the pastor and asked if there was verse in the Bible that had those words. He said; "yes".

> If my people, which are called by my name, shall humble themselves, and pray, and seek my face, and turn from their wicked ways; then will I hear from heaven, and will forgive their sin, and will heal their land.
> 2 Chronicles 7:14

I then knew there was work to be done. I

called all my siblings who at this time were
screaming, crying, believing our mother was
gone. It took a lot of bold talk to get the boys
under control for them to hear what I had to
say to them. We all went to my house with my
husband, knelt down and prayed. You see
God shows up when you think it is all over. I told
my siblings they were to PRAISE GOD - not to
pray for our mother (just as I had been
instructed). After many hours of praising, we
were all at peace – knowing that God was in
control of the situation.

My husband went back to the hospital with a
cassette player to play some Christian music
for her – believing that she would at least hear
it. There were Christian nurses who were silently
praying for our mother as well. The ward was
filled with onlookers who felt sorry for us. In the
morning whilst washing the plates, I told God I
had done my bit and it was now up to him to
do his. I thanked him for the word he gave me
the previous day. I praised God, exulting him
for who he is and God suddenly replied me
saying, ''because I AM THAT I AM. (Exodus
3:14). I give you your mother back.''

I rushed to tell my husband what I had heard
and as we were still praying, the phone rang.
The ward was in turmoil as my mother had
woken that morning and asked for me. She

was as perfect looking as she was before she went into coma and she had asked for a cup of tea (her favourite drink).

I cannot recall how I got to the hospital to see a radiant mother who was so happy to see all her children gathered around her. She did not remember what had happened. Even my pastor was astonished. The onlookers then asked what religion we were, as they were certain our mother would be dead that morning. I thank God that after that our mother moved in with me and my family, she had another one year before the Lord finally called her home at age 62 years. God is forever faithful and he will do whatever he says he will do. Ours is to follow His instructions and trust in him – Amen.

# CHAPTER TEN

## THE MISSING RING
## AND OTHER MIRACLES

I believe strongly in the principle of first fruits, especially in tithing (as I said in a previous chapter) and the obedience of God. I would encourage many to be strict with their tithing – and if possible, to pay all tithes by direct debit to the church account. This is to ensure that you pay regularly. I believe strongly that this is an essential key that would secure the 90% (remaining income) and bless you as well. It is the only part of the Bible where God asks us to test him, bring our offering to the storehouse, and see if he will not bless us.

> And thither ye shall bring your burnt offerings, and your sacrifices, and your tithes, and heave offerings of your hand, and your vows, and your freewill offerings, and the firstlings of your herds and of your flocks:
>
> Deuteronomy 12:6

Based on scripture, I tend to remind God that I have paid my tithe anytime I lose something dear to me. I recall when my mum was alive; I used to admire a ring she had which was with initial '0' the first letter of her name. I used to beg her to give it to me but she refused as it was what she bought with cash, as a gift, on her first visit to New York - and as such, it had great significance to her. My mother wore the ring all the time. I was therefore bewildered when after she died the hospital gave me all her belongings but the ring was not amongst her personal items.

## GOD KNOWS EVERYTHING

I asked the hospital but they said that there was no other item to give me. I was shocked to think someone would have stolen such an item off my mum.

On the first anniversary of my mother's death, I was thinking of her and then I remembered her ring. The phone rang and I picked it up. The Co-op Funeral Company had looked after my mother's body before being flown to Nigeria. They said there was something for me to pick up. I went the next day and they gave me a small case and inside it was a ring. The same ring that I had asked my mum to give me – I stood there wondering why it would suddenly turn up after one year. Moreover, I was surprised why this would happen when I was thinking about it. I just concluded that this could only be God's miracle. He sees our hearts and knows our desire. What is relatively funny is that I have not even worn the ring after four years. Well – I will just keep it.

**GOD SPEAKS IN VARIOUS WAYS**
An incident that keeps my heart beating with joy was when I lost two different earrings at different times. It is amazing how I found them. The first earring was a set and I had gone to a party and worn the earrings in August. When I got home that day, I realised I had one earring missing. I was quite upset as it was part of a set with a necklace and was bought for a particular outfit. In December, I brought out the outfit to wear and then remembered that I had lost one of the earrings to go with the set. I remember speaking to God that he should not forget that I pay my tithe so I should not be losing anything. I wore another earring and went out.

I usually park my car at the same spot everyday (on a drive). On this particular day, as I was about to enter the car, I noticed something on the ground. It was my earring, which I had lost. I had driven over it many times yet it had not broken - but it was bent and I was able to pull it back to shape. This is a typical example, which shows that God cares about everything we desire or want; and cares about all that belong to us. He also hears us when we speak to him.  Just imagine; I spoke to God in December, and found the earring that I had lost four months earlier. If I had not said anything, the earring may still be on the drive. Wonderful - God reacts to our words. I believe that God would like us to communicate with him regularly concerning every need.

14 Because he hath set his love upon me, therefore will I deliver him: I will set him on high, because he hath known my name.

15 He shall call upon me, and I will answer him: I will be with him in trouble; I will deliver him, and honor him.

Psalms 91:14 &15

**ANOTHER MIRACLE**
This interesting incident happened in my bedroom (so I thought). I sometimes take off my earrings and put them under my pillow when I am about to sleep.  Therefore, one day, I went to bed and put my earrings under my pillow. The next day, I could find only one earring under my pillow and was sure the other

had fallen near the bed. I searched everywhere and could not find it. Again, I reminded God of his promise to protect us and ours as – having paid my tithe.

About a week later, my daughter who is always in a hurry and walks like a soldier, came to me with my earring - saying she found it on the ground at the Tram station near our house. I know it is only God that could have made her see this – knowing that she is not one to look on the ground whilst walking. Moreover, she walks so fast that I tend to ask her to slow down so I can catch up with her whenever we are walking together.

This single event has been a great encouragement to me – making me to consistently believe in the greatness of God. God is the Alpha and the Omega - the only one and great God. The one I have decided to put all my trust in. The one that has NEVER let me down. He is a miracle working God.

**WHAT'S NEAR OUR DOORSTEP?**
The sweet miracles in my life continued one evening. On collecting my daughter from school, - she must have been about six or seven years old then. Rather than walk into the corridor to get to our flat, she stood by the door looking down at something. I moved her

shoulder so I could see what was so fascinating to her that she could not speak when I asked her to keep going. It was a snake with its head raised up and coiled right by the entrance door, which was open. It was as though it was waiting for someone. My first instinct was to pick it up and show my daughter saying - "see it's a toy snake, they don't have snakes in London.'' Instead, I pulled my daughter to myself and we dashed through the entrance past the snake and rushed to wake my husband who was asleep in the sitting room.

He thought it was an imaginary story or a joke. As our daughter kept saying what we had seen, he took a hammer, wore Wellington boots with trousers tucked in and went to the corridor entrance. The snake was still there with its head raised. My husband killed it; but how do you explain this to anyone - that it is possible to find a snake just like that in London? Only those who see the snake will believe your story; God is faithful in his protection.

> Yea, though I walk through the valley of the shadow of death, I will fear no evil: for thou art with me; thy rod and thy staff they comfort me.
> Psalms 23:4

# CHAPTER ELEVEN
## A UNIQUE EXPERIENCE

As I have stated earlier, I believe my ministry is in giving. It is therefore not surprising that at my church, the Holy Spirit led me to give a couple some money. I decided in my mind that I would give them two hundred pounds only; but the Holy Spirit intervened and said I should give them five hundred pounds. I obeyed God and gave the couple the money. This is a couple whom I did not know what they were going through or whom they were - but obedience to God's instruction is vital to me. Moreover, when you see the result, you become aware or in awe of the awesomeness of God.

The couple later called me (after a few days of enquiring of my name and phone number) and testified that they had rent due of five hundred pounds and had no way of paying it. They were going to ask someone to give them the money but God told them not to. They were so grateful for my obedience to God. On the week that I gave the money, I realised that I was left with only ten pounds. This would last me until that Friday when I would be paid my salary. By Thursday, I had no money for lunch so I emailed some work colleagues to bless me with lunch stating that God said if you do it to one of these, you have done it to me. I immediately got enough money to buy lunch.

**OUTBREAK OF BLESSINGS**
As I came back from buying my lunch, I got an email to say that as a volunteer first aider at my workplace, they had decided to pay me five hundred pounds, which would be in my account the following day. I was still gob smacked when we were called to a meeting at work. I was informed at the meeting to head a department – a sudden promotion. I went to the toilet, knelt down and thanked God. I was really touched and moved - wondering how quickly God rewarded my obedience.

That same week, my accountant told me to expect a cheque from Inland Revenue for one thousand, seven hundred pounds - as I had overpaid my tax. I got the cheque – praise God.

A few weeks later, my brother decided to bless me with an air ticket to travel abroad to Canada – more rewards of obedience to God.

When God wants to do something massive in your life, he will request for ALL you have and if you look at this and say "NO I cannot give ALL – saying ''what will I live on''? Then you have missed your blessing. God knows – you do not have to tell him.  He knows that it is all you had before asking you to give it up. This issue of giving has developed my faith strongly as I know he will never leave me nor forsake me – and he will provide all my needs – Amen.

The main thing is to know that it is God who is requesting you to carry out specific instructions – and you need faith to carry the instruction through. As you lean on God through your faith and prayers, you will get your breakthrough. Amen.

> But my God shall supply all your need according to his riches in glory by Christ Jesus.
> Philippians 4:19

# CHAPTER TWELVE

## THE CHRISTIAN LIFE IS NOT A BED OF ROSES

It is easy to read through these testimonies and imagine that it has always been smooth and easy with me. Some may even think that God has been pouring out abundance of material things on me at all times, and that I must be the happiest person on earth every second of the day. It is necessary to show the other side of the coin so that we would learn to appreciate the fact that the Christian life is not a bed of roses.

**THE GRACE OF GOD IS SUFFICIENT**
It is only the grace of God that has seen me through these many years – only the power of God has kept me until this day. It was not easy to deal with the issue of burying my mother who was 62, only to bury my brother who was 30 three months later. The Bible says trials and tribulations will come; the question is how do you deal with them when they come?  Whom

do you turn to? This is what will determine whether all the testimonies in previous chapters will happen in your life.

The problems that I have had in life have made me cling to God more and more. For those of you who have not been married, I would use my life to encourage you to be yoked with a Spirit-filled man that loves God. Seek to be friends primarily and seek God's view on the man. Also, listen to the words of your parents – not neglecting their sound advice – thinking that they are old.

As the first born of my parents, my father brought me up with words that still ring in my ears - "What a man can do, a woman can do better". Knowing this, I have strived to work hard, and at the same time prayed and believed that God would lift my husband to a high estate. That is what Christian women should do – pray for the prosperity of their husbands.

**KEEPING HUMBLE IN PROSPERITY**
My initial experience of my marriage was not very interesting – but God has taught me to pray for my marriage in order to avoid the sort of problems that we had – which are common in the initial aspects of most marriages. Moreover, pray that you do not earn more

than your husband, or that if you do, it would be handled with a lot of humility and wisdom. Not all men would like the woman to be in financial control of the family; but it is possible that there are men who would not want to progress into being the head of the family financially. This could bring much rift to a relationship, and as a result if badly handled, doors may be open to outsiders who are ever ready to listen and give all sorts of suggestions and advice. Moreover, one should be shutting such doors and not opening them.

I thank God for blessing my marriage. In my early years of marriage, I invited as many as would hear what our problems were, to listen; but I have learnt my lessons and I give thanks to God. After twenty years of marriage, I have a few advice for many. Firstly, the grace of God has been bountiful on our behalf. God has been the one carrying us through out these years.  My belief is that if God blesses you and you are faithful to God and your husband, you will be able to overcome all temptations along the way. Moreover, God will do a divine work in your spouse in spite of any unresolved issues or negative characteristics in him.

I have seen the greatness of God manifested in my husband and I give thanks to God for the years that I invested in praying for him. I am now reaping joy, companionship, communication and PEACE. Praise the name of Jesus.

There will be incidents in your Christian life that would challenge you a great deal. Moreover, in your relationship with various Christians, be careful not to equate being born again with being just religious. God has no room for religious people; they are only religious and not transformed within. I am saying this because there are many out there who do not have deep Christian witness.

## A FRUSTRATING EXPERIENCE

You have to know that people will say many negative things about you – but keep your ears open to God's voice. At a particular time, a wrong impression was given to somebody about me; I therefore foolishly thought of taking my own life because of what was said about me and how it was said. How could I have destroyed what I did not create? God in his goodness, love and mercy led me to a Christian woman – late at night – who prayed with me. I had to forgive the person who offended me so I could have spiritual freedom to continue in life.

What is interesting is that God prepared somebody to minister to me at that particular moment. Not too many people would even think of going to talk to a spirit filled Christian in such a situation – not even when God lays it on their mind. Moreover, Christians should be careful not to act on impulse in all circumstances. It is important to seek the mind of God concerning any situation.

I tend to see that experience as a spiritual attack – like many others that I have faced in life; and I thank God that he spared my life and opened my eyes to the fact that there is power in the blood of Jesus. Furthermore, God is always creating a door of escape for me from the traps of the evil one.

I have come to realise that as Christians, our faith will be tested. Ever imagined waking up in the morning and seeing fine cut lines on your body? I recall that I have had to get deliverance, as my arms will be bleeding because of attacks from the enemy in my sleep. It was as if a new blade had been used to cut marks on my body. What was even frustrating was that it would be thought that you used your fingernails to hurt yourself in your sleep - but I had not touched a blade nor had I scratched myself. I give God the Glory that I am here today to testify about this.

Let them be ashamed and confounded
together that seek after my soul to destroy it;
let them be driven backward and put to shame
that wish me evil.

Psalms 40:14

# CHAPTER THIRTEEN
## WARNING ABOUT AN ACCIDENT
## AND BETRAYAL

A former work colleague appealed to me to hire her to assist me at my new work place. Seeing that she was very desperate, I agreed and she started work with me some weeks later. I also made a pledge to God that I would provide monthly food money to her sister's son who needed support until he finished high school. He was about 15 years old then.

I took the first amount for that month and was on my way to work. I was praising God and just worshipping him when I heard God say "You are about to have an accident.'' I was still pondering this when I heard a loud bang. The car behind me had run into my car. I was calm and continued to praise God as I stepped out of the car to see what damage had been done. To God be the glory, there was not a dent in my car. The occupant of the other car, a woman – was full of apologies, as her baby had distracted her attention. Her car was dented. She profusely apologised and I told her that it was fine and went back to my car and drove off.

As I stepped into the office, I called my colleague and gave her the boy's lunch money for the month. She was rather shy but thankful. I continuously gave that money for the boy's lunch till the boy finished high school.

Whilst all this was happening, my colleague had decided to move up the ladder by backstabbing me to my bosses - to a point where she was promoted above me. For the next few years, she made my life a misery at work. She would recommend that I was not paid any bonus despite my hard work and long hours at the office. I was questioning God - asking what is happening to me. I also wondered why she would do such a thing to me. I can only say that it was the grace of God that kept me at the workplace as I dreaded going to work.

27 But I say unto you which hear, Love your enemies, do good to them which hate you,
28 Bless them that curse you, and pray for

them which despitefully use you.
Luke 6:27 &28

It will surprise you to know that one day, the announcement came that my colleague had been sacked unceremoniously because of abuse of office.
My message in this is that God would not allow those that you have blessed to be a thorn in your flesh, and be used by the evil one to destroy you. With your eyes, will you see the reward of the wicked in the land of the living. Amen. It is not impossible to see those who wish you evil falling into the trap that they set for you.

> And Moses said unto the people, Fear ye not, stand still, and see the salvation of the LORD, which he will shew to you to day: for the Egyptians whom ye have seen to day, ye shall see them again no more for ever.
> Exodus 14:13

# CHAPTER FOURTEEN
## "I WANT YOU TO BUILD A SCHOOL"

The year of 2005 was named as a year of celebration. In November as I was praying, God told me to build a school in Nigeria for underprivileged children. I knew this was God's instruction as it was not something I would willingly do. That same day, God told me that the land would be given to me. In January 2006, a preacher said if God has asked you to do something, you had better get on with it.

Like any other person, I started looking to buy land. Firstly, I had forgotten that the land was supposed to be given to me (as God had revealed to me) and secondly, I did not even have the money to buy the land.

**AN OPEN DOOR**
On 31st January, I decided to phone my father to wish him 'Happy New Year'. As I spoke to him, I asked if he had contacts to sell land, as I wanted to buy land in Nigeria. He then asked me where I wanted to buy the land, I said not

at Ile Ife - which is where my father lives. He was quiet and then said; "could it be because of you that I have been going through my recent hustle and bustle in the past two days?" I asked him what he meant and he said that he just suddenly decided to get some hired labourers to clear a piece of land he had since 1985. He was baffled with himself as to why he was clearing a land he had abandoned for such a long time – wondering that he neither wanted to sell it nor build on it.

He said to me that four acres of land had been cleared and that it was available to me if I wanted it – free of charge. The phone went dead not because my dad dropped the phone but because I pressed a knob in error out of shock. The last place I felt I would get the land was from my father. To start with, I did not even know he had the land and secondly our relationship had strained since my mother's death.

## MORE OPEN DOORS

Out of amazement at what was going on, I mentioned the incident to my boss at work and he decided to ask the global head if Deutsche Bank could sponsor me in fund raising to get the school built. The answer came back positively and since then, a committee named "Project Nigeria" was set up where we meet fortnightly to arrange fundraising ideas.

I know it can only be God at work when a woman stopped me at my work place doorstep and wanted to sell me raffle tickets for building a school at Ile Ife, Nigeria. She was not aware that what she was doing had originated with me at the bank. In the process of attending fund raising, I have attended functions where even my bosses at work can only dream of attending. I have been in halls, which can only be described as amazing. I have attended banquets and functions given to the banks high class clients where we (the committee) have been allowed to sell raffle tickets to raise funds.

> If any man serve me, let him follow me; and where I am, there shall also my servant be: if any man serve me, him will my Father honor.
> John 12:26

In the course of one year, we have raised twenty one thousand pounds out of the forty thousand pounds needed to build the school. For every pound that a bank staff pays or spends on a raffle, the bank matches the amount. Praise God. Hallelujah.

# When **God** Speaks

The Charity "God's Children Empowered Ltd" was registered in the UK within 3 weeks, a process that normally takes 3 – 6 months to get approval. Since this project was set up, I have had offers of free land (anywhere in Oyo state in Nigeria) to build a school. This is how God works. I strongly believe that God will give you a small project to test you – and see how you fare with it; then he would place something bigger in your care if you are faithful.

Five years ago, I was sponsoring four children in Gambia for their education; it never dawned on me that God would instruct me to build a school. I was also led to donate money for six years (monthly) to assist one of my pastors to build a school in Zambia called Kings College for underprivileged children. At that time, I never thought I would be doing the same thing myself. God willing, and by his grace, we hope to open the school in September 2007. It will be in memory of my late mother whose name 'Omolade' befits the whole essence of the project; meaning - children are 'a crown', 'a joy' - children are precious.

# CHAPTER FIFTEEN

## WHEN GOD SPEAKS
## LISTEN AND OBEY

As this book gradually draws to an end, it is important to mention the following points – especially for those who really seek to hear the voice of God and walk according to his will.

- You cannot physically do anything to earn God's love. It all starts with John 3:16. Read and meditate, or think deeply about the verse. Let it minister to you.

- You need to have faith and believe in Jesus Christ and he will do the rest. Furthermore, God does not expect you to pass an exam or a test to be accepted into his kingdom.

- When Adam and Eve sinned, man became subjected to death, illness, hard labour, etc. Praise God for Jesus who died on the cross, rose again and now intercedes for us in the presence of God the father.

- Salvation does not come by merit; God has freely given salvation to humankind. Your part is to accept that Jesus died on the cross to set you free.

- Ask for forgiveness of sins and invite Jesus to come into your life. In so doing, you start an everlasting exciting relationship with Christ.

- Seek to hear God's voice. God speaks to us in various ways. In my personal experience, he speaks to me through: **(a)** visions **(b)** dreams **(c**) direct inward speech and **(d)** through ideas and impressions on my mind. However, it makes sense to confirm what God says with his word and the words of God's chosen people.

- Most times when God shows you a vision, or talks to you, he may not show you the whole issue or picture. As you obey in the little he has shown you, he will then reveal more and more to you. This in turn will make you get closer to God and more dependent on him.

- Getting close to God can be achieved through praise and worship, prayer, pleading the blood of Jesus, and meditation on the word of God. (see Joshua 1:8), and learning to be alone with God through personal devotion with God.

- In all the spiritual experiences stated above, the crucial factor is to be born again. The only true way to God is through Jesus; Jesus is the way. (see John 14:6).

- Only those who are born again will enjoy the spiritual experiences highlighted in this book and understand the message that God wants to put across.

- No matter what sins you have committed, God will erase all that history in a flick of an eye as long as you (a) repent and (b) invite him into your life. It is only then that you would be ready for this exciting adventure that I have been blessed to share with you.

- If you believe and you are ready, say the following prayer with me:

# When **God** Speaks

**Dear God, I repent of all my sins, I ask you to forgive all my sins. Lord Jesus, I believe you are the son of God, thank you for dying on the cross to set me free. I ask you to come into my heart and I know that my life will never be the same again - Amen.**

- It is as simple as that. If you have said these words meaningfully, and you really want a change in your life, then sit back and see the life changing events that will take place in your life.

- Now that you have become a born again Christian, desire to seek God first. Spend time worshipping God. You may even start by listening to Christian worship music. Read the Bible. As you do this, pause and listen for the voice of God - be still for a while to hear what God wants to say to you after worshipping him.

- Keep a pen and paper beside you as it is good to write what you hear; in order to remember and secondly to confirm the events happening in the future. This is how God reveals his word to us and we can then share the experience with others as a form of testimony.

- You need to fully and totally trust God and have an unwavering faith – you must do whatever God instructs you to do, no matter how silly or enormous the task appears to be. Always confirm with the word of God.

- If you will humble yourself, God will speak clearly to your heart. Take a flash back to the testimonies and how God revived my mother from a coma even when the doctors had written her off.

- The devil will use close friends to try to make you doubt what you heard from God; do not be discouraged. Their negative views will not change what God has spoken to you. Look again at the testimony about the house that I shared. Those people still own that house now – for more than ten years.

- As long as you know that you have support from the word of God, stick to the voice of God and do not be moved concerning any revelation that God gives to you.

- It is very important to have a very powerful spiritual base – meaning a local church; and you must be active and develop a good relationship with an understanding and caring pastor – they can be very good spiritual parents. Your pastor will support you with prayers and guide you through periods of spiritual problems or attacks.

- The devil does not like those who obey God's instructions; but God loves such people. You will overcome ALL obstacles if you follow the instructions of God as outlined in the word of God – the Bible. Moreover, set your mind on Jesus through the word of God in the Bible.

- It is important to publicly acknowledge what God has done in our lives and truly glorify his name. Your testimony may be an encouragement to someone out there that may be going through one problem or the other, or having problems with a venture or assignment. Do not be ashamed of the gospel of Jesus – tell others about the Lord.

# When **God** Speaks

> Whosoever therefore shall be ashamed
> of me and of my words in this adulterous
> and sinful generation; of him also shall
> the Son of man be ashamed, when he
> cometh in the glory of his Father with
> the holy angels.
> Mark 8:38

- When God is not speaking to your heart,
  it does not mean that he has forsaken
  you. Check that you have not swayed
  from him - go ahead and do all that is
  right for the kingdom. Sit back and relax
  – wait for the next task God has for you.
  The Holy Spirit knows when to prompt
  you to move. It is therefore not
  uncommon to be woken up by the Holy
  Spirit at a specific time everyday for a
  whole week to pray or listen to God
  speaking to you and giving you
  instructions.

## A PRAYER FOR YOU - THE READER
Dear God, my great father, I pray for all those
who have read this book up to this extent. Fill
all gaps in their lives, open all blocked doors,
and make a way where there seems to be
none. I pray for the love of God and protection

of the Holy Spirit upon them - that you would give them an amazing dose of faith to embark on even more spectacular adventures in life than I have experienced and done by God's grace. I pray that they may be a blessing to others, carry out great tasks for your kingdom, and by so doing, testify that you are a loving and living God. Amen.

# CHAPTER SIXTEEN
## CONCLUSION
### An Exaltation of my maker

I give thanks and praises
To my everlasting comforter,
The **I am that I am**, (Exodus 3:14)
The one who said - "let there be,"
And it happened –
The world was formed.

I give thanks and praises
To my faithful, loving God,
To the one who died on the cross for my sins,
To the one who rose again from the dead
To the one who is in heaven, making
intercession for me -
My loving Jesus.

I give thanks and praises
To a very real and living God,
To the one in whom I can trust,
To the one who says,
"Rise up; your sins are forgiven."
The one who clothes the naked,

# When **God** Speaks

The one who watches over me
day and night - who says,
"Be still and know that I am God."

I give thanks and praises to my God.
To God, my healer;
The one who sorts out situations
Even when we fall through naivety.
To the God who sees my heart and said',
"Because I Am that I Am, I give you your
mother back."

I give thanks and praises
To God, who lifts me up, and takes
me out of the hands of my enemies.
Who makes a way where there is no way.
To an awesome God,
To a God who in the still of night would
touch you with loving kindness;
I give all thanks.

I give thanks and praises
To God, in whom all things are possible,
To God that enables me to live,
Live from day to day.
My God of miracles -
My God, who speaks all the time.